A TRUE BOOK™

Physical Science
Electricity
and
Magnetism

CODY CRAN

D1275512

Children's Press®
An Imprint of Scholastic Inc.

Content Consultant
Valarie Akerson, PhD, Professor of Science Education
Department of Curriculum and Instruction
Indiana University Bloomington, Bloomington, Indiana

Library of Congress Cataloging-in-Publication Data
Names: Crane, Cody, author.
Title: Electricity & magnetism / by Cody Crane.
Other titles: Electricity and magnetism I True book.
Description: New York : Children's Press, [2019] I Series: A true book I Includes bibliographical references and index.
Identifiers: LCCN 2018034481I ISBN 9780531131374 (library binding) I ISBN 9780531136003 (pbk.)
Subjects: LCSH: Electricity—Juvenile literature. I Magnetism—Juvenile literature.
Classification: LCC QC527.2 .C73 2019 I DDC 537—dc23
LC record available at https://lccn.loc.gov/2018034481

All rights reserved. Published in 2019 by Children's Press, an imprint of Scholastic Inc.
Printed in North Mankota, MN, USA   113

SCHOLASTIC, CHILDREN'S PRESS, A TRUE BOOK™, and associated logos are trademarks and/or registered trademarks of Scholastic Inc.

Scholastic Inc., 557 Broadway, New York, NY 10012

1 2 3 4 5 6 7 8 9 10 R 28 27 26 25 24 23 22 21 20 19

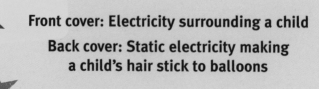

Front cover: Electricity surrounding a child

Back cover: Static electricity making a child's hair stick to balloons

Find the Truth!

Everything you are about to read is true *except* for one of the sentences on this page.

Which one is **TRUE**?

T or F Batteries make electricity.

T or F Magnets stick to plastic objects.

Find the answers in this book.

Contents

THE BIG TRUTH!

Current Showdown

Magnet holding paper clips

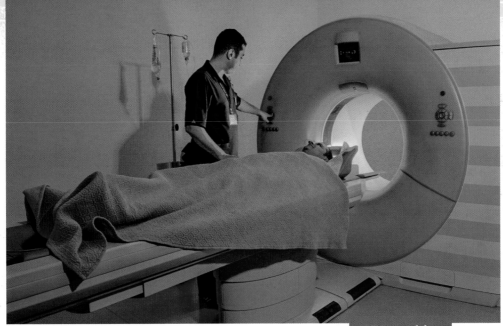

MRI machine

4 Useful Tools

How are magnets important
in our everyday lives? **35**

Electric dog

Think About It!

Look closely at the photo on these pages. What do you notice about the image? What do you think is going on? Once you have some predictions about *what* is happening, think about *how* it is happening. What might cause what you see in the photo to occur? What evidence in the photo supports your explanation?

Stumped?
Want to know more? Turn the page!

Electricity pioneer Nikola Tesla invented the plasma ball in 1894.

Ball of Lightning

If it looks like the girls in the photo are touching tiny bolts of lightning . . . well, guess what? They are! The girls are playing with a device called a plasma ball. It is made up of a clear glass sphere filled with gases. At the center of the sphere is a metal **electrode** that gives off electricity.

Electricity zips from the electrode to the girls' fingertips when they touch the ball's surface. The electricity heats the gases as it passes through. The hot gases glow, creating zigzagging beams of light. The same thing happens when lightning strikes during a thunderstorm.

The image on pages 6 and 7 shows many of electricity's amazing properties. You'll read more about them in this book.

A lightning strike usually lasts less than a second.

Thomas Edison invented the modern lightbulb in 1879.

Electricity powers the flashing lights and billboards in New York City's Times Square.

It's Electrifying!

Our modern world runs on electricity. This energy powers our cities, our homes, and our schools. Every time you switch on a light, watch TV, or talk on a phone, you are using electricity. We rely on this energy source for just about everything we do. Imagine all the things—from refrigerators to computers—that wouldn't work without electricity!

Charged Particles

What exactly is electricity? It is a form of energy that can build up in one place and flow to another.

Electricity begins inside atoms. These tiny particles are the building blocks of everything in the universe. Zoom in on an atom and you'll find **electrons** orbiting around its center, or nucleus. Electrons have a negative charge. It is this charge that creates electricity.

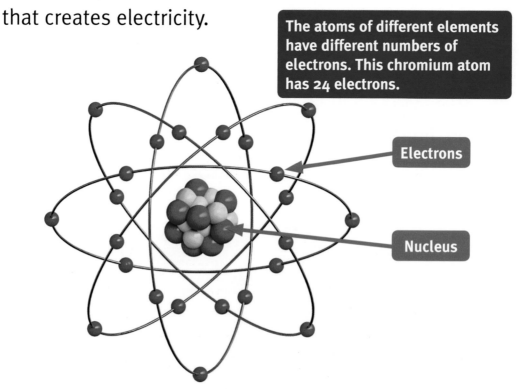

The atoms of different elements have different numbers of electrons. This chromium atom has 24 electrons.

Electrons

Nucleus

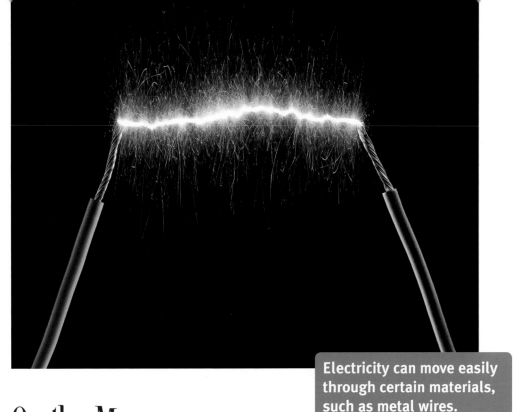

Electricity can move easily through certain materials, such as metal wires.

On the Move

Electricity needs a buildup of negative charges in order to work. That means it needs a lot of loose electrons. Electrons are knocked free when energy is added to atoms. Objects that have opposite charges attract. As a result, positive charges on nearby atoms pull the freed electrons toward them. This movement of electrons from one atom to another creates electricity.

Making Electricity

The electricity we use every day is made inside power plants. Most power plants burn fuels such as coal or natural gas to produce heat. The heat boils water, creating steam. The steam pushes against blades on large, fan-like wheels

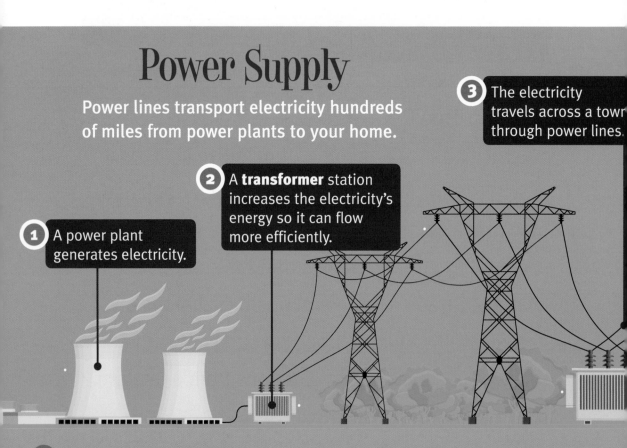

Power Supply

Power lines transport electricity hundreds of miles from power plants to your home.

3 The electricity travels across a town through power lines.

2 A **transformer** station increases the electricity's energy so it can flow more efficiently.

1 A power plant generates electricity.

called turbines, making them spin. The turbines are connected to **generators** that spin with the turbines. As the generators turn, they change their energy of motion into electrical energy. Other plants use flowing water, wind, earth's heat, or the sun's energy to power a generator.

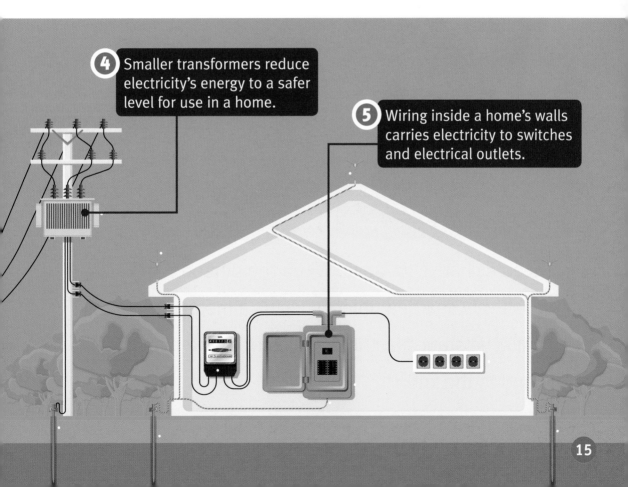

4 Smaller transformers reduce electricity's energy to a safer level for use in a home.

5 Wiring inside a home's walls carries electricity to switches and electrical outlets.

Rubbing a balloon on your head creates static electricity that causes your hair to stand on end.

Static Electricity

We can make electricity in power plants. But it also occurs naturally as static electricity. This can happen if a person wearing socks shuffles across a carpeted floor, for example. As the person's feet rub on the carpet, the socks collect electrons. Those excess electrons just need a chance to move. When the person touches a positively charged object such as a metal doorknob, ZAP! The static electricity jumps from the person's hand to the knob.

KABOOM!

Lightning is another example of static electricity, but on a much bigger scale. Lightning occurs when electrons build up at the bottom of clouds. This gives the clouds a strong negative charge. The ground below, though, has a strong positive charge. The opposite charges attract, and electrons rush from the sky to the ground. This transfer happens in an instant. You see it as a flash of lightning!

Lightning strikes Venezuela's Lake Maracaibo more often than any other place on Earth.

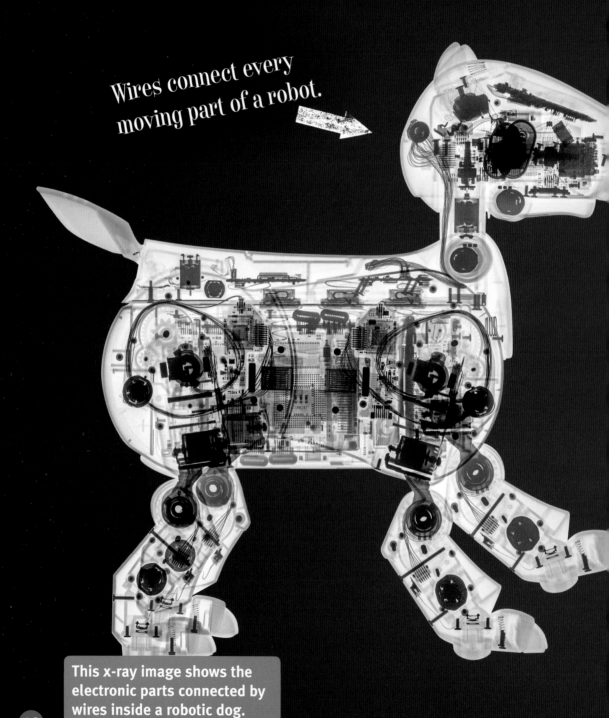

Wires connect every
moving part of a robot.

This x-ray image shows the
electronic parts connected by
wires inside a robotic dog.

CHAPTER 2

Electric Currents

Electronic devices need a steady stream, or **current**, of electricity to run. Their energy source cannot just appear and disappear in a flash the way static electricity does. A current flows into an appliance when it is plugged into an electrical outlet. Wires carry the electricity into and throughout the machine, powering its parts. This continuous supply of energy keeps refrigerators cooling, hair dryers blowing, and radios playing.

Batteries have a positive (+) end and a negative (-) end. Different sizes supply different levels of current.

Battery Pack

A battery produces an electric current on the go. It is like a tiny, portable power plant. Alessandro Volta, an Italian scientist, created the first modern battery in 1800. He stacked plates of zinc and silver, with saltwater-soaked paper in between each plate. The metals and saltwater reacted, allowing electrons to flow through the battery to create electricity. Today, batteries are found in countless devices, from cell phones to flashlights.

Energy Loop

Electrical currents only flow if they have a complete loop of wires and connections. This path is called a **circuit**. In the example below, a wire connects a battery to two lightbulbs. Electrons from the battery flow through the wire to the bulbs, lighting them up. Another wire from the bulbs carries the electricity back to the battery.

Opening the switch in the circuit breaks the connection, stopping the flow of current and turning the bulbs off. Closing the switch completes the circuit. It allows the current to flow freely and bulbs to continue shining.

HOW A CIRCUIT WORKS

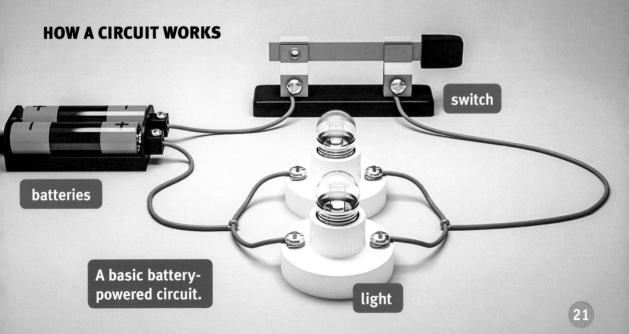

switch

batteries

A basic battery-powered circuit.

light

Conductors

Electricity can move through some materials but not others. Metals, for example, are good **conductors**, which means electricity passes through them easily. Why? Electrons can break away from metal atoms without difficulty. The loose electrons are free to move through the material. For this reason, wires in electrical cords and circuits are made from metal.

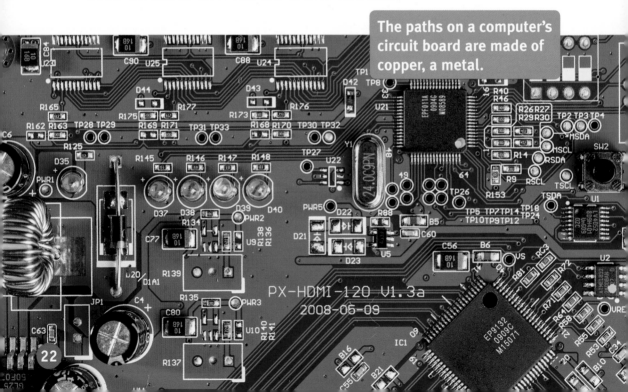

The paths on a computer's circuit board are made of copper, a metal.

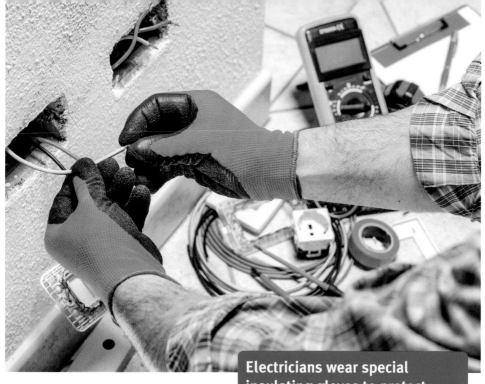

Electricians wear special insulating gloves to protect themselves from being shocked.

Insulators

Electricity does not flow well through plastic, wood, or rubber. They are good **insulators**. The atoms in these materials hold tight to their electrons. Insulators are used to cover electrical devices, wires, and power outlets. Power cords have a plastic coating that keeps you from touching the metal wires inside. They allow people to handle these objects without the risk of getting a shock.

Current Showdown

Toward the end of the 19th century, people were still looking for safe and efficient ways to bring electricity into homes and businesses. In the 1880s, two inventors came up with opposing solutions.

Direct Current (DC)

- Current flows in one constant direction
- Some electricity is lost with distance
- Current's strength cannot be increased or decreased
- Modern example: Batteries

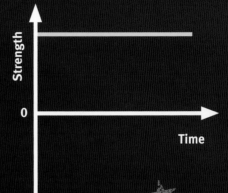

Strength

0

Time

Thomas Edison

Thomas Edison developed direct current (DC). Nikola Tesla created **alternating** current (AC).

Edison and Tesla were locked in a bitter battle over which method was best. It became known as "the War of the Currents." In the end, AC won. It is the method we still use today to carry electricity over long distances.

Alternating Current (AC)

- Current's direction switches back and forth several times per second
- Can travel over long distances and lose little power
- Current's strength can easily be increased or decreased
- Modern example: Power outlets in buildings

Nikola Tesla

Magnets can be found in nature in rocks called magnetite.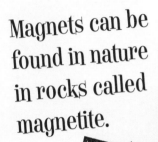

Most people have magnets holding up notes and pictures somewhere in their home.

CHAPTER 3

Magical Magnetism

Magnets can do some amazing—and mysterious—things. They are not sticky like glue or tape. Yet they can hold tight to certain objects. Magnets can also move some materials without even touching them. There's nothing really magical about magnets, though. Science can explain their strange powers! Magnets push and pull on objects because they give off an invisible force. This force is called magnetism.

The Right Stuff

Magnets can only be made of certain metals, such as iron, cobalt, or nickel. And they only interact with these same metals. A magnet will stick to a nail because nails are made mostly of iron. Magnets will not attract objects made of glass, plastic, or wood. Try touching a magnet to various objects around you and see what happens. This can help you figure out what materials make up these objects.

How Magnets Work

Just like electricity, magnetism comes from electrons. In addition to their electric charge, these particles act like teeny-tiny magnets. The atoms in most materials are arranged so their electrons' magnetism pulls in different directions. As a result, their forces cancel one another out and the material does not act like a magnet. But in a magnet, the atoms' electrons all pull in the same direction. That pulling power combines to create a strong magnetic force.

A magnet pulls on putty that has powdered bits of iron mixed into it.

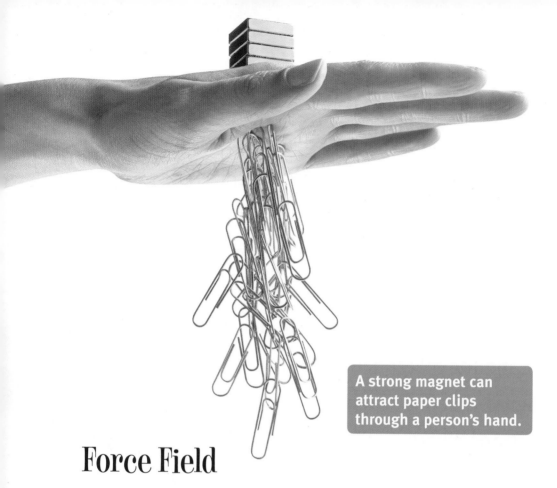

A strong magnet can attract paper clips through a person's hand.

Force Field

A magnet's force forms an invisible **magnetic field** around its source. When objects near the field, they're pushed away or pulled toward the magnet. A magnetic field can pass through materials. It can push and pull objects with the same force even if there is a barrier between them and the magnet. The bigger or stronger a magnet is, the larger its force field is.

Push and Pull

The force of a magnet is strongest at the magnet's two ends. These are called the north and south **poles**. In the same way positive and negative charges attract, opposite poles attract. The north pole of one magnet and the south pole of another are pulled together. The opposite happens when two north poles or two south poles of magnets come close. They **repel** each other, pushing the magnets apart.

Iron filings show the magnetic field that pulls the opposite poles of two magnets together.

Electricity Makes Magnets

In 1825, British scientist William Sturgeon coiled a wire around a piece of common, non-magnetic iron. When he sent electricity through the wire, the iron became a magnet. The iron returned to being non-magnetic when Sturgeon turned off the electricity. This experiment created the world's first electromagnet. These magnets can be turned on and off, like a lightbulb.

Timeline of Discovery Through the Ages

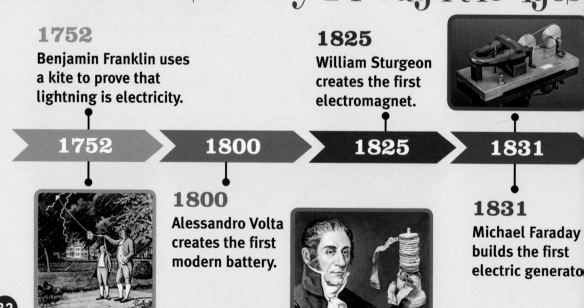

1752
Benjamin Franklin uses a kite to prove that lightning is electricity.

1825
William Sturgeon creates the first electromagnet.

1752 ▶ **1800** ▶ **1825** ▶ **1831**

1800
Alessandro Volta creates the first modern battery.

1831
Michael Faraday builds the first electric generato

Magnets Make Electricity

Six years later, another British scientist discovered that magnets can also make electricity. Michael Faraday placed a copper disk between the north and south poles of a horseshoe magnet. When he spun the disk, electricity flowed through it. This was the first electric generator. Today, power stations use huge spinning generators to make electricity.

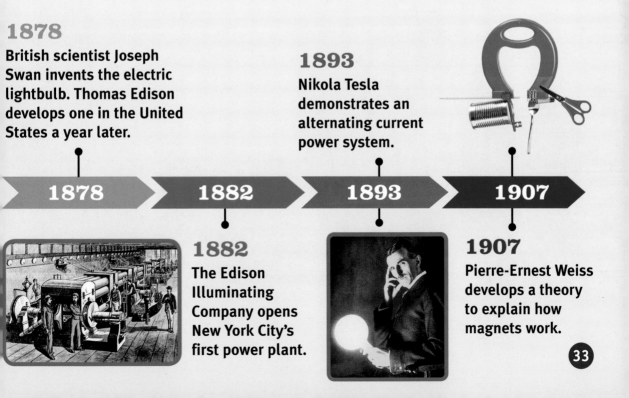

1878
British scientist Joseph Swan invents the electric lightbulb. Thomas Edison develops one in the United States a year later.

1893
Nikola Tesla demonstrates an alternating current power system.

1882
The Edison Illuminating Company opens New York City's first power plant.

1907
Pierre-Ernest Weiss develops a theory to explain how magnets work.

1878 — 1882 — 1893 — 1907

Powerful electromagnets help move scrap metal at junkyards.

A range of devices, from doorbells to speakers, use electromagnets.

Useful Tools

You might not realize it, but there are magnets all around you. Many can openers grip cans with the help of magnets. Magnetic screwdrivers hold on to screws as they turn. Credit cards use a magnetic strip to transmit information when swiped. Vibrating magnets inside speakers turn electronic signals into sound. Cars use magnet-driven motors to power features such as wipers and windows. And that's not all!

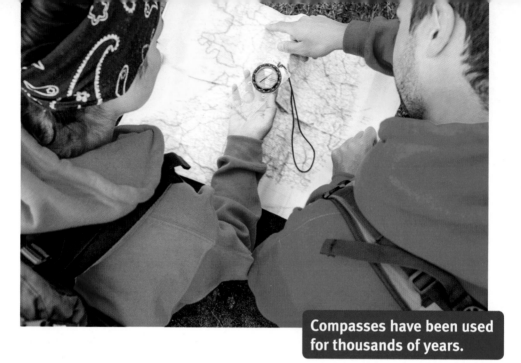

Following Directions

Airplane pilots, sailors, and hikers all rely on compasses to find their way. A compass has a magnet shaped like a needle at its center that can rotate to point in any direction. The needle always points north no matter which way a person turns. A person can position a map so its symbol for north faces the same way the compass points. This helps the person figure out which direction he or she needs to go.

Earth's Magnetic Field

A compass works because Earth has its own magnetic field. Our planet is actually a giant magnet! Earth's core is made mostly of iron, some of which is melted. Earth spinning on its axis and heat inside the core cause the liquid metal to swirl. The flow creates electric currents, which produce Earth's magnetic field.

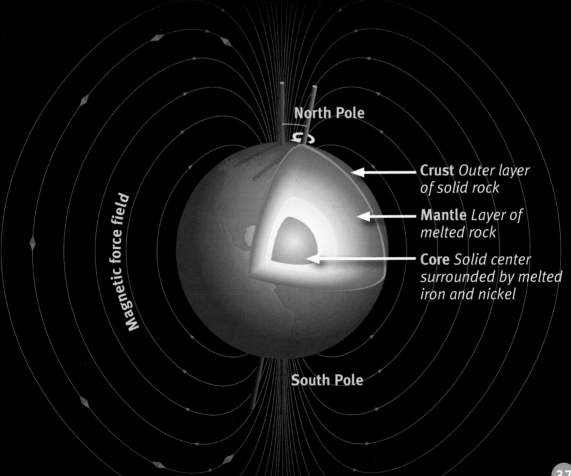

North Pole

Magnetic force field

Crust *Outer layer of solid rock*

Mantle *Layer of melted rock*

Core *Solid center surrounded by melted iron and nickel*

South Pole

Flying Trains and Lifesaving Images

A maglev train can move at superfast speeds. A metal coil runs the length of the train's track. The coil becomes a powerful electromagnet when electricity flows through it. It repels large magnets in the bottom of the train, causing the train to float above the track. Since maglevs do not roll along the ground the way typical trains do, there is little to slow them down. Instead, maglev trains fly along on a cushion of air.

A maglev train floats just a few inches above its track.

The fastest maglev train can travel at 375 miles (604 km) per hour.

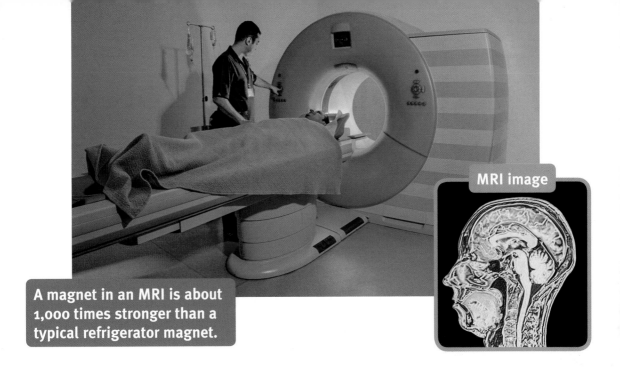

A magnet in an MRI is about 1,000 times stronger than a typical refrigerator magnet.

MRI image

Doctors can look inside a patient's body using an MRI (magnetic resonance imaging) machine. A ring containing several strong electromagnets passes over a person. The magnets are so strong that atoms in the person's body react to their pull. A computer measures these reactions and uses them to form three-dimensional images.

These are just some of the countless ways magnets and electricity help us every day. Look around you. What other examples can you spot? ★

Shocking Static!

How does static electricity build up enough of a charge to shock you? Try this activity to learn more.

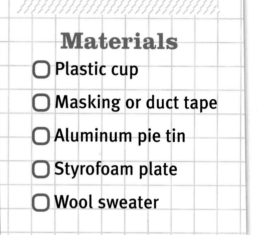

Materials
- ☐ Plastic cup
- ☐ Masking or duct tape
- ☐ Aluminum pie tin
- ☐ Styrofoam plate
- ☐ Wool sweater

Directions

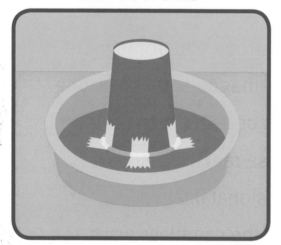

1. Tape the cup upside down to the center of the pie tin.

2. Quickly rub the bottom of the Styrofoam plate against your hair or a wool sweater for 1 minute.

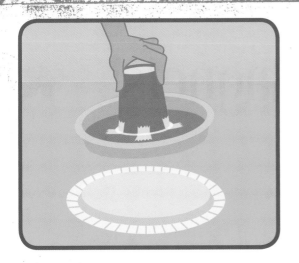

3. Set the Styrofoam plate upside down on a flat surface. Without touching the pie tin with your hands, pick it up by the cup and set it down on top of the plate.

4. Slowly touch your finger to the pie tin. What do you feel?

5. Try this experiment again in a dark room. Watch closely when you touch the tin. What do you see?

Explain It!

Using what you learned in this book, can you explain what happened with the pie tin? If you need help, turn back to page 16 for more information.

Floating Magnets!

As magnets attract and repel one another, their movements can look like magic. Learn a few tricks with this activity.

Materials

- 6 small ring magnets
- Drinking straw
- Modeling clay

Directions

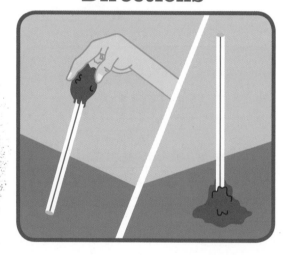

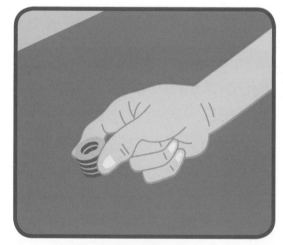

1. Mold the clay around one end of the straw to form a base. Stick the clay to a flat surface so the straw stands upright.

2. Stack four of the ring magnets so they stay together. Slide them onto the straw.

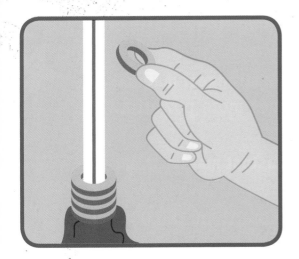 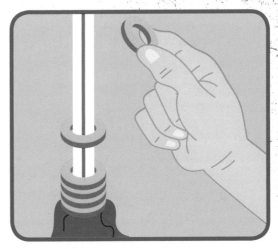

3. Slide one remaining magnet onto the straw. If it sticks, flip it over and try again. What happens?

4. Slide the remaining magnet onto the straw. What happens? If you flip the last magnet over, what changes?

Explain It!

Using what you learned in this book, can you explain what happened with the magnets and why? If you need help, turn back to page 38 for more information.

True Statistics

Number of times lightning strikes Earth every day: 8 million

Strength of the world's strongest magnet: About 50 million times more powerful than Earth's magnetic field

Speed of the world's fastest maglev train: 375 mph (604 kph)

Speed of electricity: More than 186,000 mi. (299,338 km) per second

The number of lightbulb designs tested by Thomas Edison: About 3,000

Number of power plants in the United States: More than 8,000

Combined length of all the high-voltage power transmission lines in the United States: More than 200,000 mi. (321,869 km)

Did you find the truth?

(T) Batteries make electricity.

(F) Magnets stick to plastic objects.

Resources

Books

Holzweiss, Kristina A. *Amazing Makerspace DIY Electricity.* New York: Children's Press, 2017.

Kulling, Monica. *Zap! Nikola Tesla Takes Charge.* Toronto: Tundra Books, 2016.

Parker, Steve. *Electricity.* New York: DK Children, 2013.

Stringer, John. *Magnetism: An Investigation.* New York: PowerKids Press, 2008.

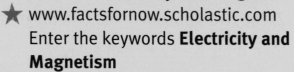

Visit this Scholastic website for more information on electricity and magnetism:
★ www.factsfornow.scholastic.com
Enter the keywords **Electricity and Magnetism**

Important Words

alternating (AWL-tur-nate-ing) taking turns

circuit (SUR-kit) a complete path for an electric current

conductors (kuhn-DUHK-turz) substances that allow electricity or sound to travel through them

current (KUR-uhnt) the movement of electricity through a cable or wire

electrode (ih-LEK-trode) a point through which an electric current can flow into or out of a device or substance

electrons (ih-LEK-trahnz) tiny particles that move around the nucleus, or center, of an atom and carry a negative electrical charge

generators (JEN-uh-ray-turz) machines that produce electricity by turning a magnet inside a coil of wire

insulators (IN-suh-lay-turz) materials that are able to stop the flow of electricity

magnetic field (mag-NET-ik FEELD) the area around a magnet or electric current that has the power to attract other metals

poles (POHLZ) the two opposite ends of a magnet

repel (rih-PEL) to drive back or push away

transformer (trans-FOR-mur) a piece of equipment that reduces or increases the voltage of an electric current

Index

Page numbers in **bold** indicate illustrations.

About the Author

Cody Crane is an award-winning children's writer, specializing in nonfiction science. She studied science and environmental journalism at New York University. Before becoming an author, she was set on becoming a scientist. She later discovered that writing about science could be just as fun as doing it. She lives in Houston, Texas, with her husband and son.